She Bloomed Through Stars And Scars

A Journey of Love, Loss, and Becoming

Shivani Pachisia

BookLeaf
Publishing

India | USA | UK

Made with ❤ on the BookLeaf Publishing Platform
www.bookleafpub.in
www.bookleafpub.com

Dedication

For every soul who has ever carried both light and
darkness, and still chose to bloom.

Preface

This book is not just mine—it belongs to every girl who has ever stood at the edge of love and loss, and wondered how to keep going. It belongs to the quiet moments when life feels heavier than our hearts, and the unexpected sparks that remind us we are still alive, still becoming.

She Bloomed Through Stars and Scars is a collection of feelings more than words—each poem born from tenderness, from ache, from wonder. It is about the beauty of growing through pain, about finding light even in the cracks, and about learning that love, in all its forms, is both fragile and infinite.

If you have ever felt broken and still dared to dream, if you have ever carried both sorrow and hope in the same breath—these pages are for you. May you find a reflection of yourself in these verses, and may you leave knowing that your own stars and scars can coexist, beautifully.

Acknowledgements

This book was born from countless quiet moments, from unspoken feelings, and from the courage it takes to turn vulnerability into words. This book is dedicated to every reader: you are the reason these pages exist. May you find yourself in these verses, and may they remind you that your stars and scars can coexist beautifully.

1. Until Forever Comes

We keep waiting
For something that may not even be worth hating.
Still, because of our weak heart, we wait—
And this foolish act becomes the harshest fact.
Our brain tells the heart to stop,
Does everything to help it cope.
But the heart, bound by its feelings,
Turns into a weakling.
It beats only in this fragile hope
That it cannot truly cope:
That someday, this wait will end—forever.
And the day will draw closer;
It won't be much longer,
For forever will seal our fate.

2. End of the Garden

I run in a bed of flowers,
as high as a tower,
that keep me running
without turning.
I feel I'm in a place
so gentle, so safe,
where I forget everything
that holds no meaning.
for it was my past,
and I knew it could never last.
So, without thinking,
I keep moving,
dancing and singing,
without looking
where it might be leading.
I can feel the wind blowing,
which increases my beating.
I want to scream so loud,
for it feels like floating
on the ninth cloud.

Swayed by the Wind
At last, I reach the end,
a place that feels
like a blend of all
I have ever dreamt.

3. The Candle Stands

I open the window,
see and hear things
I don't even want to know.
Still, with my eyes wide open,
I stare—
a painting so rare,
one that could be beautiful
if only we care.
I keep struggling
to reach the inner core
of something vanishing
day by day,
and someday will remain no more.
But all I am left with
is hope—
the only thing that helps me cope.
I am not myself anymore.
I am not what I want anymore.
Yet the changing seasons
give me endless reasons

why I should survive
and fight
for what is my birthright.
I don't want to be the rose
that withers when all doors close.
I want to be like the candle—
burning, flickering, melting,
and still, with all its strength,
it stands.
Every bad has an ending,
and every good, a beginning.
This is why my heart
doesn't stop beating:
in the hope of a safe landing—
one that feels far,
but not as far as the star.

4. The Path of Needles

With every sun rising,
my heart keeps on crying.
I watch the sun set
with my eyes so wet.
Between these two beautiful phenomena
I try to cross paths,
a tired and bruised loner
with a heart still bleeding.
I walk this path full of needles,
hearing my heart—so faint, so feeble.
The storm keeps increasing;
still I move forward,
my eyes blinking,
not letting my steps be overpowered.
I feel the rashes,
my body full of scratches;
but ignoring them,
I glimpse the end's flashes.
As I keep crossing,
I see and learn new things—

lessons so engrossing.
I am neither safe nor secure,
I have no friend, nor a foe;
yet I keep moving, learning
that the mistakes I made
are not worth repeating.
The people I chose
are not worth caring.
I see their ungratefulness,
I feel the shallowness—
which deepens my heart's feebleness.
With my look so tattered
and my heart so shattered,
I keep moving straight
to change my fate,
to leave behind everything
that's happened till date.
And still I move,
without stopping.
I see my end—
the only way
for my heart to mend.

5. Heaven in Hell, Hell in Heaven

I've seen heaven in hell,
and hell in heaven.
I've seen castles made of sand,
and people losing all their land.
I've seen birds flying out of cages,
and life turning into mazes.
I've seen people hide their tears,
their hearts overflowing with fear.
I've seen faith slowly decay,
and love twisting into hate.
I've seen love sold for money,
and backstabbers faking loyalty—
which is never funny.
I've learned to expect the unexpected,
how the smallest things
leave a life affected.
I've seen relationships break,
and tears turn ponds into lakes.
I've seen a rat fall for a snake,

and a child admiring a cake.
I've seen lies hidden behind every truth,
and trust uprooted
at each stage of youth.
I've learned to sharpen my senses,
to cross all kinds of fences.
I've learned to believe in myself,
to break the shell,
to face every form of hell
To prepare for the future
without any booster,
and reach the end—
without stopping at any bend.

6. Between the Devil and the Deep Blue Sea

I lie on the bed
and look at the walls,
a picture of memory
etched and engrossed.
A memory so light,
bringing nonstop rain,
fading at the speed of light—
yet still there,
like a particle in my brain.
A beautiful lie
I try to hide,
yet it lingers,
residing in my eyes.
Come close to me,
feel my pain,
and you will know
the reason for the rain.
Why do I feel so cold?
Why is my heart so stoned?

Where is the warmth
that should wrap me
like a piece of cloth?
Why is the girl lost in the woods,
searching for a path,
hiding under her hood?
Where is her guide
to show her the way?
Where is the ride
to carry her away?
Why must she inhale the air,
so full of mud and dust?
It feels so unfair.
She looks at the falling star
in the dark night,
searching for the light
in every rising tide.
She just walks,
fearing what she sees:
on one side the devil,
the other—the deep blue sea.

7. The Reap of Time

In a prison
full of reasons,
not a single person
who is certain.
We can see,
yet remain blind,
full of glee,
but still so bland,
on this land
where time runs
out of hand—
like sand.
We are running so fast
that nothing we do
will truly last.
And still I wonder:
how to join the links,
to know when
I will reap

the fruits of all
my varied deeds.

8. The Gate and the Bait

Life is all about
give and take.
Life is all about
love and hate.
Life is all about
the chase and the wait.
Life is all about
the rate and the date.
Life is all about
reaching the gate,
for which we must find
the hidden bait—
which may come fast,
or may come late.
So wait,
and see
what your fate has to say.

9. Stream of Dreams

I flow in a stream,
a current of dreams,
that makes me scream —
for this is what binds me to the beam,
the beam of hope
that helps me cope
with the hardships of the slope
I long to climb, to reach the top.
It helps me sort
through the mesh of tangled thoughts,
the ones that slow me down —
turning me into a sloth.
Thanks to the stream and the beam,
that shimmer and gleam,
soothing my soul like gentle cream,
and keeping alive my tender dream.

10. Us Against the World

I hate you, I love you—
my heart skips a beat without you.
You may not know,
but my heart
knows only to love you.
And sadly,
that's all it knows.
My heart's truth,
my reality,
is just you.
I need you, I want you—
an intensity I can't show you.
Can you stay alone?
Or can you not?
Let's hold hands
and find the sun's warmth—
Us against the world,
that's all I want.
Can we not be the one

and tell the world,
bring it on?

11. A Girl I Know

A girl I know,
whose life feels like a bore.
She wakes from sleep
and knows only how to weep.
She is scared to see
what her future holds,
a path unknown,
a story yet untold.
She wants someone
who truly understands her,
someone to stand beside her.
She feels so low,
wishing the world could know
she is not always what she shows.
She feels suffocated
in a world so restricted.
She longs to be independent,
not dependent,
to rise above the burdens,
to cross every hurdle.

She wants to be free—
and yes, carefree.
She has dreams to fulfill,
giving her the will
to climb every hill of life.
And yes, I am sure,
for this journey is mine.

12. The Road I Walk

I walk on a road
where not a single soul exists.
It's just me and my goal.
I keep walking,
without stopping,
lost in thought:
What does my life truly want?
Where is it heading?
What will be its conclusion?
It's so confusing—
I don't know who it will be,
I don't know who I will become,
I don't know what I will be.
This road holds so many mysteries,
sparking endless curiosities,
sometimes making me ferocious,
reminding me that life is precious,
full of surprises
that make it utterly melodious.

13. Lost in the Night, Found in Love

Twinkle in her eyes,
she gazes into the night,
dreaming of a miraculous light.
The moon glows soft and bright,
casting its warmth upon her delight.
She reaches for a star —
so close, yet so far.
Could it be her knight,
lost somewhere in the night?
Her heart whispers softly,
hoping love will find its way,
to shine upon her
and never fade away.

14. The Heart You Stoned

The rain is pouring,
the droplets trickling.
The windowpane so unclear—
I can't see a thing, but I hear
the stormy night's thunder,
the darkness slowly creeping.
Your soul is freezing,
the goosebumps increasing
with each strike of lightning.
The lonely path,
the gloomy heart—
it's so hard to accept
that nothing lasts.
The road, so full of puddles,
increasing the hurdles,
drenched by the water splashes,
the careless passersby so ignorant
of the rashes.
Am I confused,
or just suffused

with the blood of the darker side, let loose?
The bloodshot eye,
love-lost sight,
the heart full of thorns,
the soul that has forgotten to mourn.
The eyes you see
are full of pain and misery—
but why would you care,
as you just stand and stare?
Now the blood is spilled,
from the soul you killed.
Feel the cold
of the heart you stoned.

15. Crossroads of the Heart

I walk in the heat,
looking at the sun,
my eyes so blinded
by people with their fake fun.
Your eyes still stare,
my beating heart can't spare
the love I gave
to a soul unaware.
A question I ask
to one who loves:
what do you feel
while wearing the mask?
Unaware of the meaning,
I stand so cold,
searching for the void within me,
still missing, still untold.
Do I hate to love,
or love to hate?
Is it vice versa,
or bound to fate?

Holding my hands,
I walk the road,
looking in the eyes,
the feeling untold.
Am I confused,
or is truth tightly glued?
Am I walking the wrong path,
searching for the end of solitude?
Breaking the barrier,
to follow my heart,
instead of the path given,
is the hardest task.
Should I end the journey,
or wait for fate's glory?
Should I return to the heart so lonely?
Why does it feel so gloomy?
How can I find the way
to the heart's crossroad,
when I walk both paths
with my spirit heavy, my heart full of load?

16. Ignite the Fire

I am giving up all I hoped for,
I am giving up all I wished for,
I am giving up all I dreamed of,
because in the end I realized
this is not what I live for.
Why not me?
Why not my heartbeat?
Why not my love?
Why not my fire?
Am I a liar?
To whom am I lying?
To whom am I proving?
My strength is just a way
to not give my life away.
Why can't I be loved?
Why can't I be the priority?
Why am I taken for granted—
is this what is destined?
For how long can I control?
For how long can I not show?

I need my support
and to be the strength
for my beating heart.
This is not what I deserve.
This is not what I want to preserve.
This is not what I stand for.
This is not what my soul asked for.
Give me my answer.
Give me my laughter.
Ignite the fire—
be the lighter.

17. Heartbeat Fluctuates

I close my eyes,
I open my eyes.
I close my eyes,
and again, open my eyes—
to see a memorable part of my life.
With eyes so intense,
and thoughts so dense,
with touch so affectionate
that my heartbeat fluctuates.
Each moment spent
makes me forget all I regret.
My days are made beautiful
with kisses so wonderful.
My knees go weak,
yet I feel nothing beneath my feet.
The person before my eyes
is someone I will never forget—
all my life.
And all that I have said is true,
for this person is you.

18. Unexpected Breeze

You came into my life
like an unexpected breeze of happiness,
a life once tangled
in events full of hassles.
With you, I feel the warmth again—
the warmth that had drifted away—
and I thank you
for this moment of brightness.
No matter where our journey leads,
no matter where our next step takes us,
the only thing that matters
is our bond so magical,
our hearts no longer sceptical.
I hope you'll be there when I need.
I hope you'll cherish the moments we seed.
I know I won't go away.
I know my heart won't sway.
I pray for the magic to stay
and for our bond to grow
with each passing day.

19. Kaleidoscope of Us

We knew each other,
but never truly felt the moments together.
We might not have known
where life would carry us, where we'd be flown.
A shift in the air made us aware
that life was giving us moments to simply stare.
No matter how complicated things are,
no matter how distant our next challenges are,
the only thing that truly matters is where we are.
Life makes its own decisions,
ones we can't always envision—
and I just hope it's not a division.
I'm happy that we met,
though the secret must be kept.
I hope the bond we share
deepens the love, the care.
I hope our journey is more than fair,
because I know no matter what, I'll be there.
I hope you have a place for me in your heart,
in such a way that, even if we part,

you'll always hold me in your thought.
I'm a kaleidoscope—
one that never loses hope.
And I will always pray
that we grow closer
with each passing day.

20. Born to Roar

Look at the sky—
you will know the heights,
the heights that can take you even higher.
I know it's difficult to find the light,
to take the flight,
but I know you have what it takes to stride.
Don't let negativity shadow your thoughts.
Don't let havoc remind you of what you've lost.
Don't be sore—you were born to roar.
Don't let go of your thunder;
stay steadfast to your core.
Leader of the army,
you are who you are—my force.

21. She is Sunshine

A lady I know,
with a heart so soft
and a soul so warm.
She has her charm,
makes you feel just like home.
She is mysterious,
and yes, ferocious.
Her eyes tell a story,
hidden beneath her outer glory.
She is not just what she shows—
she is what my heart knows.
A promise I make
to her and this connection:
I'll be there,
by her side,
no matter the destination.
Long live our love, our friendship,
our bond, and memories so fond.
She is the sunshine, she is the rain;

she is my friend,
and that will remain.